BONSAI FOR BEGINNERS

*A Complete Guide to Growing, Caring,
Display, and Long-lasting*

Richard D. Reese

Copyright

Disclaimer

The information provided within this book is for general informational purposes only. While the author and the publisher have tried to ensure the accuracy and completeness of the information contained in this book, they assume no responsibility for errors, inaccuracies, omissions, or any inconsistency herein. Any slights of people or organizations are unintentional.

The views expressed in this book are those of the author alone, and should not be taken as expert instruction or commands. The reader is responsible for his or her own actions.

Adherence to all applicable laws and regulations, including international, federal, state, and local governing professional licensing, business practices, advertising, and all other aspects of doing business in the US, Canada, or any other jurisdiction is the sole responsibility of the reader or purchaser. Neither the author nor the publisher assumes any responsibility or liability whatsoever on the behalf of the purchaser or reader of these materials.

Table of Contents

Introduction

The Art of Bonsai: History and Significance

Welcome to the wonderful world of bonsai, a practice that marries horticulture and art, patience and skill, tradition and creativity. Bonsai is more than simply growing miniature trees; it's a journey of personal growth and understanding, a way to connect with nature on a deep level, and a means to cultivate tranquility and mindfulness in our busy lives.

The term 'bonsai', which translates to 'planted in a container' in Japanese, captures the essence of this art form but barely scratches the surface of its depth and complexity. A bonsai is not a genetically dwarfed plant but rather a regular tree that has been meticulously pruned and shaped to remain small while mimicking the form and scale of full-sized trees.

The history of bonsai dates back over a thousand years. The practice originated in China, where it was known as 'penjing', around the 6th century. It was originally associated with Taoism and was used as a means to express the harmony between man, nature, and the universe. The art was later exported to Japan, where it was embraced by Zen Buddhists and evolved into the form we know

1

today. Over centuries, it has been refined into a series of distinct styles and aesthetics that reflect the natural beauty and diversity of trees in the wild.

Bonsai is significant for many reasons. It is a form of living art that changes with the seasons and grows over the years, reflecting the transient and evolving nature of life itself. It also encapsulates many philosophical and aesthetic principles, such as wabi-sabi (the beauty of imperfection and transience), and yugen (a sense of deep, mysterious beauty). Bonsai also serves as a therapeutic hobby that cultivates patience, attentiveness, and a deeper appreciation for nature's intricacies.

As you embark on this journey of learning the art of bonsai, you will not only gain a new hobby but also a new perspective on life and nature. This book, "Bonsai for Beginners: A Complete Guide to Growing, Caring, Display, and Long-lasting," is designed to guide you every step of the way, from choosing your first tree to advanced techniques for maintaining and displaying your bonsai. It's an exciting journey, and we're delighted to be your guide. Welcome to the world of bonsai.

Why Bonsai? The Benefits and Pleasures of Bonsai Cultivation

Bonsai cultivation, a practice steeped in tradition and artistry, offers a unique and rewarding experience to anyone open to its allure. At first glance, the appeal of bonsai may seem to lie purely in its aesthetic value – the creation of a miniature yet realistic representation of a full-sized tree. However, delve a little deeper, and you'll discover a multitude of reasons why people around the world find pleasure and benefit in the art of bonsai.

1. **Connection with Nature:** Bonsai allows for a profound connection with nature, even within the confines of your own home. It's a hands-on way to engage with the cycle of life, observing the seasonal changes in your miniature tree and the intricate dance of growth and decay. Bonsai fosters an appreciation for the quiet beauty and resilience of nature.

2. **Mindfulness and Relaxation:** The practice of bonsai is a form of mindfulness, requiring focus and presence. The careful pruning, shaping, and care that bonsai requires can be meditative, providing a quiet respite from the fast-paced stresses of everyday life. Many practitioners find bonsai cultivation therapeutic and calming.

3. **Artistic Expression:** Bonsai is often referred to as "living sculpture." Through the shaping and styling of a bonsai tree, you have the opportunity to express your creativity. Each bonsai tree is unique, reflecting the vision and style of its creator.

4. **Intellectual Stimulation:** Bonsai is a continually learning process. From understanding the biology of different tree species to mastering the various techniques of pruning, wiring, and potting, bonsai offers a wealth of knowledge for the curious mind.

5. **Sense of Achievement:** Growing and maintaining a bonsai tree requires patience and dedication. Over time, as your tree starts to take shape and flourish, you'll experience a sense of accomplishment. This is a reward that grows as your bonsai does.

6. **Community and Culture:** When you delve into bonsai, you become part of a global community of enthusiasts. This community is a place to share experiences, learn from others, and even engage in friendly competition. Furthermore, bonsai provides a connection to the rich histories and cultures of China and Japan where this art form originated.

In essence, bonsai is not just about growing miniature trees; it's a lifestyle that brings numerous benefits and pleasures. Whether it's the tranquility it brings, the creativity it nurtures, or the knowledge it imparts, the art of bonsai offers a fulfilling and enriching journey to all who embark upon it.

Part I: Understanding Bonsai

Chapter 1: What is Bonsai?

As we embark on this journey into the captivating world of bonsai, it's crucial to start with a fundamental understanding. So, what is bonsai? In its simplest definition, bonsai is the art of cultivating miniature trees in pots or containers, a practice that requires careful and meticulous attention to the tree's growth, shape, and overall aesthetic.

The term "bonsai" itself originates from the Japanese words "bon," meaning tray or pot, and "sai," meaning tree or plant. Therefore, "bonsai" translates literally to "tree in a pot." However, this simple translation belies the depth and complexity of this ancient art form.

While a bonsai is indeed a tree grown in a pot, it's far more than that. Bonsai is not about dwarfing trees or stunting their growth but rather about carefully guiding and nurturing a tree to create a miniature, yet authentically proportioned, representation of nature. The goal of bonsai cultivation is not merely to create a small tree, but to evoke the spirit and aesthetic of a mature tree as it might be found in nature.

The bonsai tree, while small in size, is intended to reflect the features and shape of its full-sized counterparts. The artist, through techniques such as pruning, wiring, and careful watering, guides the tree's growth, encouraging it to develop a thick trunk, a well-structured branch system, and an overall shape that is pleasing to the eye. The result is a living piece of art that continues to grow and change with each passing season and year.

It's important to note that bonsai is not a specific type of tree. Almost any tree species can be used for bonsai, provided it can thrive in a confined space and respond well to the pruning and shaping techniques used in bonsai cultivation. The choice of tree species often depends on the aesthetic the artist wishes to achieve and the local climate conditions.

Bonsai is a practice steeped in tradition and respect for nature. It is a way to bring the beauty of the natural world into our homes and urban spaces, a miniature tableau of nature that can be appreciated up close. It's a practice that requires patience, dedication, and a keen eye for detail, but the reward is a personal and intimate connection with a living, growing piece of art.

As we delve deeper into the following chapters, we will explore the various aspects of bonsai cultivation, from choosing the right tree and pot to mastering the techniques of pruning and shaping. This journey will equip you with the

7

knowledge and skills to start your own bonsai journey and experience the many pleasures and benefits this art form can bring.

Chapter 2: Different Styles and Sizes of Bonsai

As you delve deeper into the world of bonsai, you'll quickly realize that not all bonsai trees are the same. The diversity in bonsai is vast, reflecting the rich array of tree species and forms found in nature. This chapter will introduce you to the different styles and sizes of bonsai, providing a foundation for your understanding and appreciation of this art form.

Bonsai Styles

Bonsai styles are broadly categorized based on the shape and growth pattern of the tree. Each style is inspired by natural tree forms and landscapes. Some of the most common styles include:

- **Formal Upright (Chokkan):** This style represents a tree that has grown in ideal conditions, with a straight, upright trunk tapering smoothly from base to apex. The branches decrease in size as they ascend the trunk, creating a symmetrical, balanced look.

- **Informal Upright (Moyogi):** As the name suggests, this style is less formal and more common in nature. The trunk is curved or twisted, but the tree's apex is still located directly

9

above the base, creating a sense of visual balance.

- **Slanting (Shakan):** In this style, the tree leans to one side, simulating the effect of wind or a heavy snowfall. The apex of the tree is not directly over the base, creating a dynamic, natural look.

- **Cascade (Kengai):** This style mimics trees that grow on steep cliffs, bending down under the force of gravity. The trunk cascades down the side of the pot, and in extreme cases, it can even reach below the base of the pot.

- **Semi-Cascade (Han-Kengai):** Similar to the cascade style, but the trunk does not drop as dramatically. The apex of the semi-cascade bonsai is generally at or below the rim of the pot but does not extend below the base.

- **Literati (Bunjin):** This style symbolizes a tree's struggle for light. The trunk is slender and contorted, with sparse foliage, often only at the top of the tree. It gives the impression of age and survival against harsh conditions.

These are just a few of the many styles found in bonsai. Each style offers a different aesthetic and presents unique challenges and rewards for the bonsai artist.

Bonsai Sizes

The size of a bonsai is another factor that varies widely. The size is typically determined by the height of the tree, from the top of the pot's soil to the tree's apex. Here are some common classifications:

- **Mame or Shohin (Miniature Bonsai):** These are small trees, typically less than 10 inches tall. They can be held in one hand and require special care due to their small size.

- **Kifu or Chuhin (Medium Size Bonsai):** These trees range from 10 to 24 inches tall. They are still relatively compact but allow for more detail and complexity than smaller sizes.

- **Dai or Omono (Large Bonsai):** These are large trees, over 24 inches tall. They can be quite impressive and require significant space and effort to maintain.

Each size category brings its unique challenges and rewards. Smaller trees may be more delicate and require more precise care, but they also allow for a miniaturized, intricate display. Larger trees can make a strong visual impact and offer more room for shaping and styling.

Understanding the styles and sizes of bonsai is the first step in choosing and shaping your own bonsai tree. As you grow in your bonsai journey, you may find yourself drawn to certain styles or sizes, and your preferences may evolve over time. The beauty of bonsai lies in this flexibility and diversity, offering endless possibilities for personal expression and growth.

Chapter 3: Understanding Bonsai Terminology

As with any specialized field, bonsai cultivation has its unique terminology. This language can initially seem daunting, but understanding it will significantly enhance your appreciation and practice of the art of bonsai.

There are many different types of bonsai trees, and each type has its own unique set of characteristics. Some common bonsai trees include pines, maples, junipers, and azaleas. Bonsai trees can be grown indoors or outdoors, and they can be kept in a variety of different sizes.

The care of bonsai trees is a complex and time-consuming process. Bonsai trees need to be watered regularly, fertilized, and pruned on a regular basis. They also need to be protected from pests and diseases. Here, we'll cover some of the most common terms you'll encounter in your bonsai journey.

- **Aerial root:** A root that grows above the ground. Aerial roots are often used to anchor bonsai trees to their pots.

- **Akadama:** A type of clay soil that is commonly used for bonsai. Akadama is porous and well-draining, which makes it ideal for bonsai trees.

- **Back budding:** A technique used to encourage new growth on older branches. Back budding is done by removing the terminal bud on a branch, which will stimulate the growth of lateral buds.

- **Bonsai:** We've touched on this, but to recap, bonsai is a Japanese term that translates as "tree in a pot" or "planted in a container." It refers to the art of cultivating and shaping miniature trees to mimic mature, full-size trees in nature.

- **Branch:** A woody stem that grows off of the trunk of a tree. Branches are used to support the leaves and flowers of a tree.

- **Bud:** A small, undeveloped shoot that will eventually grow into a leaf, flower, or branch.

- **Cambium:** A layer of tissue just beneath the bark of a tree. Cambium is responsible for the growth of new cells in the tree.

- **Canopy:** The topmost branches and leaves of a tree.

- **Deadwood:** Dead wood that is left on a bonsai tree to create a natural and aged appearance.

- **Fertilizer:** A substance that is added to soil to provide nutrients for plants. Bonsai trees need to be fertilized regularly to maintain their health and vigor.

- **Girdling:** A technique used to kill a branch or trunk by cutting off its bark. Girdling is sometimes used to remove unwanted branches or to create a more natural-looking bonsai tree.

- **Grafting:** A technique used to join two plants together. Grafting is sometimes used to combine the desirable characteristics of two different plants.

- **Hardwood cutting:** A cutting that is taken from a woody stem. Hardwood cuttings are typically taken in the fall or winter.

- **Nebari:** Nebari refers to the visible surface roots of a bonsai tree, spreading out from the base of the trunk. Good nebari is desirable as it gives the impression of age and stability.

- **Jin:** A jin is a part of the tree, usually a branch or part of the trunk, which has been stripped of bark to simulate a dead or broken branch, adding an impression of age and struggle.

- **Shari:** Shari is similar to jin but refers to a section of the main trunk that has been stripped of its bark. This technique is used to create the impression of a tree aged and weathered by the elements.

- **Apex:** The apex is the topmost part of the bonsai tree. In most bonsai styles, a well-developed and well-defined apex is crucial as it contributes to the tree's balance and symmetry.

- **Wire Training:** This is a technique used in bonsai to shape and guide the growth of the tree. By carefully wrapping wire around branches, you can manipulate their direction and angle to achieve the desired shape.

- **Pruning:** Pruning is the act of selectively removing parts of the tree, such as branches, buds, or roots. This is done to control the shape and size of the tree, encourage growth in specific areas, or maintain the overall health of the tree.

- **Repotting:** Repotting is the process of removing the tree from its pot, pruning its roots, and then replanting it in the same or a different pot. This is typically done to refresh the soil, manage the tree's size, or change the aesthetic of the tree-pot combination.

- **Yamadori:** This term refers to a tree collected from the wild. While many bonsai are grown from seeds or cuttings, collecting mature trees from nature is another common practice.

- **Suiseki:** While not a bonsai term per se, suiseki is closely related to the bonsai world. It is the Japanese art of stone appreciation, often with stones displayed in the same way as bonsai.

- **Shaking:** A technique used to remove dead leaves and debris from the soil of a bonsai tree. Shaking is also used to aerate the soil and improve drainage.

- **Shari:** A technique used to create deadwood on the trunk of a bonsai tree. Shari is done by removing a strip of bark from the trunk, which exposes the dead wood underneath.

- **Style:** The overall appearance of a bonsai tree. There are many different styles of bonsai, each with its own unique characteristics.

- **Substrate:** The material that is used to fill a bonsai pot.

This list is just the start, and there are many more terms to learn as you delve deeper into the art of bonsai. Don't be overwhelmed by the new terminology. Instead, see it as a pathway to understanding and appreciating the subtleties of this profound and rewarding practice. As you become more familiar with these terms, they will become a natural part of your bonsai vocabulary and enhance your understanding and practice of this beautiful art form.

Part II: Getting Started with Bonsai

Chapter 4: Choosing Your First Bonsai Tree

The moment has arrived – you are ready to choose your first bonsai tree. This is a significant milestone in your bonsai journey, and understandably, it can be a little daunting. This chapter will guide you through the process, offering tips and considerations to help you make the right choice for your first bonsai.

❖ Understanding Your Commitment

Before you choose your first bonsai tree, it's crucial to understand the commitment you are about to make. Caring for a bonsai tree requires consistent attention and care. It's not just a plant; it's a living piece of art that you are committing to shape, guide, and nurture.

As a bonsai cultivator, you will need to regularly water your tree, check its health, prune its branches and roots, and periodically repot it. The specific care requirements will depend on the tree species and the environment in which it is growing. Remember, bonsai cultivation is not about instant results. It's a long-term commitment that rewards patience and steady care.

❖ Choosing the Right Species

Choosing the right species for your first bonsai tree is crucial. As a beginner, you'll want a species that is relatively easy to care for and resilient to common mistakes. Some species recommended for beginners include:

1. **Juniper (Juniperus):** Junipers are hardy trees that are well-suited to bonsai cultivation. They are resilient, adaptable, and respond well to pruning and wiring.

2. **Ficus (Ficus):** Ficus trees are tropical and prefer warm climates. They are particularly suitable for indoor bonsai and are known for their root structures, which can be trained into appealing shapes.

3. **Chinese Elm (Ulmus parvifolia):** Chinese Elms are versatile trees that can be grown indoors or outdoors in most climates. They have small leaves and a robust growth habit, which make them ideal for bonsai.

When choosing your tree species, consider the growing conditions you can provide. If you live in a cold climate, a tropical tree like a Ficus may not be the best choice unless you can provide it with a warm indoor environment.

❖ Buying vs. Growing

As a beginner, you might wonder whether to buy a pre-established bonsai tree or start from a seed or cutting. While growing a bonsai from seed can be rewarding, it's a very long process and requires advanced skills. As a beginner, it's usually best to start with a pre-established tree. This will allow you to start practicing the techniques of bonsai care and styling right away.

❖ Inspecting the Tree

When choosing a bonsai tree, you'll want to inspect it carefully to ensure it's healthy and has good potential for further development. Here are some things to look for:

1. **Trunk:** The trunk should be thick and taper towards the top, giving the tree a balanced and mature appearance.

2. **Branches:** Look for well-distributed branches all around the trunk. The branches should decrease in size as they ascend the trunk.

3. **Roots:** The roots, or nebari, should be visible at the soil surface and spread evenly around the base of the trunk.

4. **Foliage:** The leaves or needles should be a healthy color, with no signs of disease or pest infestation.

❖ **Buying from a Reputable Source**

Finally, make sure to buy your first bonsai tree from a reputable source. Good bonsai nurseries and suppliers will have healthy, well-cared-for trees and knowledgeable staff who can provide advice and guidance.

Choosing your first bonsai tree is an exciting step. Take your time, do your research, and remember that bonsai cultivation is a journey, not a destination. Each tree is unique and will grow and develop in its own time. Your role as a bonsai cultivator is to guide and nurture your tree, helping it achieve its full potential as a living work of art.

Chapter 5: Essential Bonsai Equipment and Tools

When starting your bonsai journey, it's vital to equip yourself with the right tools. Quality tools not only make the job easier but also ensure that you can care for your bonsai effectively, minimizing damage and stress to the tree. This includes providing them with the right amount of water, fertilizer, and sunlight, as well as pruning and training them to maintain their desired shape and size. In addition to proper care, you will also need a few essential tools to help you with your bonsai hobby. Here is a list of the most important bonsai tools:

1. Pruning Shears:

Also known as bonsai scissors, these are a must-have in your bonsai toolkit. You'll use them to prune leaves, small branches, and roots. Bonsai shears come in various sizes. However, a medium size is versatile enough for most beginners.

2. Concave Cutters:

A concave cutter is a specialized tool that allows you to make precise cuts that heal with minimal scarring. It's used for removing branches and creating jins (artificially aged-looking deadwood). The unique concave design leaves a hollow wound that heals more naturally over time.

3. Wire Cutters:

Bonsai wire cutters are used to remove wires wrapped around the branches without damaging the tree. They have a rounded tip that allows you to cut close to the trunk or branch.

4. Bonsai Wire:

Bonsai wire is used to shape and train the branches and trunk of your bonsai. Aluminum and copper are the most commonly used materials, with aluminum being more suitable for beginners due to its ease of use and flexibility.

5. Root Hook:

A root hook is used during repotting to gently disentangle the root ball, helping to prevent unnecessary root damage. Single or multiple-pronged root hooks are available, with the choice depending on the size and complexity of your bonsai's root system.

6. Bonsai Turntable:

A turntable, or rotating bonsai stand, makes working on your bonsai much easier. It allows you to easily turn the tree to work on it from different angles without having to lift or potentially harm the tree.

7. Watering Can or Hose with a Fine Nozzle:

Watering is a crucial part of bonsai care. A watering can or hose with a fine nozzle ensures that water is delivered gently to the soil, avoiding any soil displacement or damage to the delicate roots of your bonsai.

8. Bonsai Soil:

Bonsai soil is different from regular potting soil. It's designed to be fast-draining while still retaining enough moisture to keep the tree hydrated. Ready-mixed bonsai soils are available, or you can learn to mix your own.

9. Fertilizer:

Like all trees, bonsai need nutrients to thrive. A balanced bonsai fertilizer should contain Nitrogen, Phosphorus, and Potassium, along with trace amounts of other essential nutrients. The specific nutritional needs can vary based on the tree species and the time of year.

10.Bonsai Pots:

Bonsai pots are not just containers but a crucial element of the overall bonsai aesthetic. They come in a range of shapes, sizes, and colors. Generally, the pot should harmonize with the tree and complement its overall design. The size and shape of the pot can also impact the tree's growth and health.

Having the right tools and equipment can make a significant difference in bonsai cultivation. Start with the basics, and as you gain more experience and confidence, you may wish to expand your toolkit. Keep in mind that proper care and maintenance of your tools will also ensure their longevity and effectiveness.

Investing in good-quality bonsai tools is investing in the health and beauty of your bonsai trees. In the next chapters, you'll learn how to use these tools and start applying the techniques of bonsai cultivation.

Chapter 6: Selecting the Right Bonsai Pot

In the art of bonsai, the bonsai pot is an important part of the overall appearance of your bonsai tree. It is an integral part of the overall composition, contributing to the aesthetic harmony and health of your bonsai. Selecting the right bonsai pot can seem complex, with numerous factors to consider. This chapter will guide you through these considerations and help you choose a pot that complements and enhances your bonsai tree.

There are many different types of bonsai pots available, so it is important to take the time to choose the right one for your tree. Here are a few things to consider when selecting a bonsai pot:

1. Size of the Pot

The size of the bonsai pot is essential for both aesthetic and practical reasons. From a visual perspective, the pot should balance with the size of the tree to create a harmonious overall appearance. A general guideline is that the pot's length should be roughly two-thirds the height of the tree. However, for very short or cascading styles, the pot should be about as long as the tree is tall.

Practically, the size of the pot directly impacts the health of your tree. A pot that's too small might not provide enough room for roots to grow, leading to unhealthy, stunted growth. Conversely, a pot that's too big might lead to waterlogging, as the excess soil can retain too much moisture.

2. Shape of the Pot

The shape of the pot should complement the style of your tree. Rectangular and oval pots are often used for formal, upright styles, as they enhance the tree's stability and grandeur. Round or freeform pots can complement informal or slanting styles, adding to the overall sense of movement and naturalness. For cascading styles, deep, narrow pots are often used to balance the long, downward branches.

3. Color and Texture

The color and texture of the pot should highlight the best qualities of your tree without drawing attention away from it. Generally, muted, earthy tones are preferred, as they don't distract from the tree's foliage and bark.

The texture can also play a role in enhancing the tree's characteristics. A smooth, glossy pot can add contrast to a tree with rough bark, while a rustic, unglazed pot can enhance the rugged appearance of a tree with jin or shari features.

4. Material of the Pot

Bonsai pots are made from a variety of materials, with ceramic being the most common due to its durability, breathability, and aesthetic appeal. Other materials include plastic (often used for training or developing trees), concrete, and various metals. Each material has its pros and cons, affecting durability, cost, and aesthetics.

5. Drainage and Wiring Holes

Healthy bonsai cultivation requires proper drainage to prevent waterlogging. Your pot should have at least one large drainage hole, and often several smaller ones for optimal drainage. Additionally, these holes are used to secure the tree with wire, preventing it from shifting or falling out of the pot.

6. Quality of the Pot

A well-made bonsai pot can last for decades if cared for properly. High-quality pots have even thickness, well-defined shapes, and sturdy, smooth rims. The glaze, if present, should be evenly applied without cracks or bubbles. A quality pot is an investment in the longevity and beauty of your bonsai.

Once you have considered all of these factors, you can start shopping for a bonsai pot. There are many different places where you can buy bonsai pots, including online retailers, garden centers, and bonsai nurseries.

Here are a few tips for choosing a bonsai pot:

- Buy a pot that is one size larger than your tree's current pot. This will give your tree room to grow.

- Choose a pot that is made of a material that is porous and well-draining. This will help to prevent root rot.

- Avoid pots with designs or patterns on the surface. These can distract from the beauty of your tree.

- Choose a pot that is the right color for your tree. The color of the pot should complement the color of your tree's foliage and bark.

With a little bit of thought and effort, you can choose the perfect bonsai pot for your tree. The right pot will help to enhance the beauty of your tree and will make it a focal point in your home or garden.

✹ Additional Information ✹

Here are a few additional things to consider when selecting a bonsai pot:

- **Potting style:** There are two main styles of bonsai pots: classical and modern. Classical pots are typically rectangular or oval in shape and have a simple design. Modern pots are more likely to be asymmetrical or have a decorative design.

- **Drainage holes:** All bonsai pots should have drainage holes to allow excess water to escape.

- **Potting soil:** Bonsai trees need a special type of soil that is well-draining and airy. You can buy bonsai soil at most garden centers or online retailers.

- **Watering:** Bonsai trees need to be watered regularly, but you should avoid overwatering. Overwatering can cause root rot, which can kill your tree.

- **Fertilizer:** Bonsai trees need to be fertilized regularly to maintain their health and vigor. You can buy bonsai fertilizer at most garden centers or online retailers.

- **Pruning:** Bonsai trees need to be pruned regularly to maintain their shape and size. You can learn more about pruning bonsai trees from a bonsai book or online resource.

Selecting the right pot for your bonsai is a careful balancing act of aesthetics and horticultural needs. It's a decision that requires thought, research, and sometimes even a little trial and error. The right pot enhances the beauty of your tree and contributes to its overall health and well-being. In the end, the choice of pot is another avenue for personal expression in the captivating art of bonsai.

Part III: Growing Your Bonsai

Chapter 7: Planting Your Bonsai: Techniques and Tips

Planting a bonsai tree is a meticulous process requiring careful preparation and technique. It's an essential step in establishing the tree's future growth and development. This chapter will guide you through the process of planting your bonsai tree, providing practical techniques and tips along the way.

1. Preparing the Pot

Before you start planting, ensure your chosen bonsai pot is clean and ready. If it's a new pot, a simple rinse should suffice. However, for used pots, a thorough clean with warm soapy water is recommended to remove any residual soil or organic matter.

Next, cover the pot's drainage holes with mesh to prevent soil from washing out while still allowing water to drain. Secure the mesh with a length of wire, creating two loops that will later serve to secure the tree.

2. Preparing the Tree

If you're repotting an established bonsai, the first step is to carefully remove it from its old pot.

Using a root hook, gently tease out the roots from the soil, taking care not to damage them. Trim the roots if necessary – this not only helps the tree fit its new pot but also encourages more vigorous growth.

If you're starting with a pre-bonsai or nursery stock, you will need to carry out initial styling and root pruning before planting.

3. The First Layer of Soil

Add a layer of bonsai soil to the bottom of your pot. This first layer will sit underneath the root ball, so its thickness will depend on the size of your tree's roots. Bonsai soil differs from regular potting soil in its ability to drain well while retaining enough moisture for the tree.

4. Positioning the Tree

Now, place your tree in the pot. Generally, the tree should be off-center for a more natural and aesthetically pleasing look. The front of the tree – the side with the most visual interest – should face forward. Use the wire loops prepared earlier to secure the tree in place, making sure it's firm but not overly tight.

5. Adding More Soil

Once your tree is secured, add more soil to cover the roots. The soil surface should be slightly below the rim of the pot, leaving room for watering.

Use a chopstick or similar tool to work the soil into the root area, ensuring no air pockets are left.

6. Watering

After planting, give your bonsai a thorough watering. This will help settle the soil and ensure the roots have immediate access to moisture. Water gently to avoid displacing the soil, stopping when water begins to flow freely out of the drainage holes.

7. Aftercare

For the first few weeks after planting, keep your bonsai in a sheltered location out of strong winds and direct sunlight. This gives the tree a chance to recover from any transplant stress and begin establishing its roots in the new pot.

Planting a bonsai tree is more than just a technical task. It's an opportunity to form a closer connection with your tree, understanding its needs and characteristics. Every tree is unique, and through the process of planting, you'll learn to adapt your techniques to suit each individual bonsai, contributing to its health, growth, and beauty. In the next chapters, you'll explore more ways to nurture and style your bonsai, deepening your skills and appreciation for this intricate art form.

Chapter 8: Bonsai Soil and Fertilizers: Everything You Need to Know

The right soil and fertilizers are the foundation for a healthy bonsai tree. They provide the essential nutrients and water your bonsai needs to thrive. This chapter will delve into the intricacies of bonsai soil and fertilizers, providing the knowledge you need to nurture your tree effectively.

1. Understanding Bonsai Soil

Contrary to what you might think, bonsai trees do not grow best in regular potting soil. Bonsai soil is specially designed to drain quickly while retaining the right amount of moisture and nutrients. This is crucial for preventing root rot and supporting healthy growth.

There are several types of bonsai soil mix, each suited to different tree species, climates, and personal preferences. These can include Akadama (a type of Japanese clay), pumice, lava rock, and other organic or inorganic materials. The right mix depends on the specific needs of your tree and the conditions in which it's grown.

2. Preparing Your Bonsai Soil

Bonsai soil can be purchased pre-mixed, or you can create your own mix. Making your own soil mix allows you to tailor the soil to your specific tree and environment. Generally, a bonsai soil mix should have a balance of water retention, drainage, and aeration properties.

Before using your soil, it's recommended to sift it to remove fine dust that can impede drainage. You can use a bonsai soil sieve for this purpose.

3. Fertilizing Your Bonsai

Just like any other plant, bonsai trees need nutrients to grow and thrive. Because bonsai trees are confined to small pots, they can quickly use up the nutrients in their soil. Regular fertilization is therefore crucial to replenish these nutrients and support healthy growth.

Most bonsai trees require a balanced fertilizer containing Nitrogen, Phosphorus, and Potassium (N-P-K). Nitrogen supports foliage growth, Phosphorus aids in root and flower development, and Potassium contributes to overall plant health.

4. When and How to Fertilize

The best time to fertilize your bonsai depends on the species and its growth cycle. Most trees benefit from fertilization during the growing season (spring to early autumn). During winter, most bonsai trees go dormant and require less or no fertilizer.

Apply your chosen fertilizer according to the package instructions. Over-fertilizing can harm your tree, causing leaf burn and even root damage. It's best to start with a lower dose and increase if necessary.

5. Organic vs. Inorganic Fertilizers

Both organic and inorganic (synthetic) fertilizers can be used for bonsai trees. Organic fertilizers release nutrients slowly, which can be beneficial for maintaining a steady supply of nutrients. They also improve soil structure over time. However, they can be more expensive and have a stronger smell.

Inorganic fertilizers are usually cheaper and have higher nutrient concentrations. They release nutrients quickly but can also leach out of the soil quickly. The choice between organic and inorganic fertilizers often comes down to personal preference.

Choosing the right soil and fertilizers for your bonsai tree is an essential part of bonsai cultivation. It requires understanding your tree's needs and providing the right balance of nutrients, water, and air. With the right foundation, your bonsai tree can grow strong and healthy, ready to be shaped into a living work of art.

Chapter 9: Watering Your Bonsai: Best Practices

Water is essential to the health of your bonsai, but effective watering involves more than just keeping the soil moist. Understanding when and how much to water, as well as the quality of the water used, is vital for a thriving bonsai. This chapter will provide a comprehensive guide to the best practices for watering your bonsai.

1. Understanding Your Bonsai's Water Needs

Different species of bonsai have different watering requirements, depending on their natural environment. Bonsai trees that originate from dry climates will need less frequent watering than those from wetter climates. The size of the bonsai, its growth stage, and the time of year can also affect its water needs.

2. When to Water Your Bonsai

A common misconception is that bonsai should be watered on a set schedule. However, the best approach is to water based on the condition of the soil. Generally, bonsai should be watered when the topsoil feels dry to the touch but before the entire soil mass has dried out.

Overwatering can lead to root rot and other health issues, while underwatering can cause your bonsai to dry out and die. Observing your tree and its responses to watering will help you gauge the best watering routine.

3. How to Water Your Bonsai

Water your bonsai thoroughly, soaking the entire soil mass. This encourages the roots to grow throughout the pot, promoting a healthier tree. Watering should be done evenly over the soil surface until water begins to flow out of the drainage holes. A watering can with a fine nozzle or a hose with a soft spray attachment is ideal for this task.

4. Quality of Water

The quality of the water you use can also affect your bonsai's health. Bonsai trees prefer slightly acidic water, which is more similar to natural rainfall. Tap water is often alkaline and can contain chlorine or other chemicals that may harm your bonsai over time. If possible, use filtered or rainwater for watering your bonsai.

5. Seasonal Watering Needs

Your bonsai's watering needs will change with the seasons. During the growing season, usually spring and summer, your bonsai will need more frequent watering due to increased growth and higher evaporation rates. Conversely, in autumn and winter, watering can be reduced as the tree's growth slows and it enters dormancy.

6. Watering During Repotting and Aftercare

After repotting, it's essential to water your bonsai thoroughly to help settle the soil and ensure the roots have access to moisture. However, avoid watering newly pruned trees immediately after pruning to allow cuts to dry and heal.

Watering is an essential aspect of bonsai care, requiring an understanding of your tree's needs and careful observation. With attentive care and the right techniques, you can provide your bonsai with the hydration it needs to thrive. In the next chapter, we will delve deeper into the aspects of shaping and styling your bonsai, the part of bonsai cultivation that truly lets you express your creativity and connection with your tree.

Part IV: Care and Maintenance

Chapter 10: Pruning and Trimming Your Bonsai

Pruning and trimming are at the heart of bonsai cultivation. These techniques not only shape the tree into an aesthetic miniature representation but also promote its health and longevity. In this chapter, we'll explore the principles, techniques, and best practices of pruning and trimming your bonsai.

1. Understanding the Importance of Pruning and Trimming

Pruning and trimming your bonsai serve several purposes. They help maintain the miniature size of the tree, shape it according to your chosen style, encourage denser foliage, and promote the tree's health by removing dead or diseased branches.

2. The Difference Between Pruning and Trimming

While often used interchangeably, pruning and trimming refer to slightly different practices in bonsai care. Pruning generally refers to the removal of larger branches to shape the tree's structure, while trimming or pinching involves cutting smaller branches and leaves to refine the tree's shape and promote denser growth.

3. When to Prune Your Bonsai

The best time to prune your bonsai depends on the species and the purpose of the pruning. Structural pruning, which involves significant changes to the tree's shape, is typically performed during late winter or early spring when the tree is still dormant. This allows the tree to heal rapidly once it enters the growth phase.

Maintenance pruning, which involves removing excess growth to maintain the tree's shape, can be done throughout the growing season.

4. Pruning Techniques

Pruning should be done with sharp, clean tools to make clean cuts and minimize damage to the tree. Start by pruning dead or unhealthy branches to improve the tree's health. Then, proceed to structural pruning, shaping the tree according to your chosen style. Always consider the tree's natural form and growth habit when making your cuts.

5. Trimming Techniques

Trimming or pinching is a more delicate task than pruning and requires careful attention to detail. Using sharp scissors or your fingers, trim new growth back to one or two pairs of leaves. This encourages the tree to produce denser, smaller foliage, enhancing the tree's miniature appearance.

6. Healing and Aftercare

After pruning, larger cuts should be treated with a healing compound, known as wound paste, to prevent disease and encourage healing. Minor trimming does not usually require aftercare.

Following pruning or trimming, monitor your tree's health closely. Avoid repotting or other stressful activities until the tree has recovered.

7. Pruning and Trimming as an Art

More than just a maintenance task, pruning and trimming your bonsai is an expression of your creativity and connection with the tree. Each cut is a decision that shapes the tree's growth and form. With time and practice, you'll develop a keen eye for shaping your bonsai and fostering its unique beauty.

Pruning and trimming are integral to bonsai cultivation. They meld horticultural knowledge with artistic vision, shaping a living organism into a representation of nature's grandeur in miniature. Through these techniques, you shape not only your bonsai but also your understanding and appreciation of this intricate art form. In the next chapter, we'll explore advanced techniques for shaping your bonsai, including wiring and the creation of jin and shari.

Chapter 11: Wiring and Shaping Your Bonsai

In the art of bonsai, wiring is a key technique used to shape and style your tree. By carefully applying wire to the tree's branches, you can manipulate their growth and achieve your desired shape. In addition, creating jin and shari can add a sense of age and character to your bonsai. In this chapter, we'll delve into these advanced shaping techniques.

1. Understanding Bonsai Wiring

Wiring is a technique used to guide and maintain the shape of your bonsai tree. By wrapping wire around the branches and trunk, you can bend and reposition them to create your desired style. Over time, the tree will set in this position, even after the wire is removed.

2. Types of Wire

There are two primary types of wire used in bonsai cultivation: anodized aluminum and annealed copper. Aluminum wire is softer and easier to work with, making it suitable for young or delicate trees. Copper wire is stronger and holds its shape better, so it's typically used for older, thicker branches or coniferous trees.

3. How to Apply Wire to Your Bonsai

To wire your bonsai, start by selecting a wire that is about one-third the thickness of the branch you want to shape. Cut a length of wire long enough to cover the branch with some excess.

Starting at the base, wrap the wire around the branch in a spiral, maintaining an angle of about 45 degrees. Ensure the wire is snug but not so tight that it digs into the bark. Avoid crossing wires, as this can damage the tree.

4. Bending and Shaping

Once the branch is wired, you can begin shaping it. Bend the branch gently into your desired shape, being careful not to break it. It's better to bend slightly and make adjustments over time rather than trying to achieve the final shape in one go.

5. Removing Wire

The wire should be removed before it starts to cut into the bark, which can cause scarring. This is usually after a few months to a year, depending on the tree's growth. To remove the wire, cut it off in sections using wire cutters, being careful not to damage the branch.

6. Creating Jin and Shari

Jin and shari are techniques used to create the appearance of age and weathering. Jin involves stripping the bark from a branch to create the appearance of a dead, bleached branch, while shari involves creating a similar effect on the trunk. These techniques should be performed carefully, as they can't be reversed.

7. The Art of Shaping Your Bonsai

Shaping your bonsai is more than a technical task; it's an opportunity to express your vision and create a unique piece of living art. It requires a keen eye, a gentle hand, and an understanding of the tree's growth patterns. With time and practice, you can shape your bonsai into a variety of styles, each with its own beauty and charm.

Through wiring and shaping, you have the power to guide your bonsai's growth and create a stunning representation of nature in miniature. It's a rewarding process that brings you closer to your tree and allows you to express your creativity. In the next chapter, we'll delve into more advanced bonsai techniques, deepening your skills and understanding of this intricate art form.

Chapter 12: Seasonal Bonsai Care Guide

Caring for a bonsai tree is a year-round endeavor. Just as in nature, your bonsai goes through cycles of growth and dormancy. Understanding these cycles and how to care for your tree in each season is vital to your bonsai's health and beauty. In this chapter, we'll explore a comprehensive seasonal care guide for your bonsai tree.

1. Spring Care

Spring is a period of rapid growth for most bonsai trees. As the weather warms and daylight increases, your tree will exit its winter dormancy and begin to grow.

- **Watering:** As growth accelerates, so will your tree's water needs. Keep a close eye on the soil moisture and water as needed.

- **Fertilizing:** Spring is the ideal time to start fertilizing, supplying your tree with nutrients for the growing season.

- **Pruning and Wiring:** As new growth appears, you can start pruning and trimming to maintain your tree's shape.

It's also a good time to apply wire for shaping.

- **Repotting:** For most species, early spring, just as the tree begins to grow, is the best time for repotting.

2. Summer Care

During the summer, your bonsai will continue to grow, although the pace may slow as temperatures peak. This is a period of maintenance and vigilance.

- **Watering:** Water needs will be high due to heat and evaporation, so frequent watering is crucial. However, avoid waterlogging the soil.

- **Fertilizing:** Continue regular fertilization to support ongoing growth.

- **Pruning and Trimming:** Regular trimming will be necessary to manage the fast growth.

- **Protection:** Protect your tree from extreme heat and strong midday sun, which can cause leaf scorch.

3. Autumn Care

As the days grow shorter and temperatures cool, your bonsai will start preparing for winter dormancy. Growth will slow, and care needs will change.

- **Watering:** Watering needs will decrease as growth slows and temperatures drop.

- **Fertilizing:** Stop fertilizing to allow your tree to prepare for dormancy.

- **Pruning and Trimming:** Light pruning can be done, but avoid major work that the tree may not have time to recover from before winter.

- **Protection:** Start preparing for winter by protecting your tree from early frosts.

4. Winter Care

Winter is a period of rest for your bonsai. Most trees will enter dormancy, with little to no growth. Care during this time is all about protection and preparation for the coming spring.

- **Watering:** Watering needs will be minimal due to dormancy and lower evaporation, but ensure the soil does not dry out completely.

- **Fertilizing:** Do not fertilize your dormant tree. The focus is on survival, not growth.

- **Protection:** Protect your tree from freezing temperatures, especially the roots. Depending on your climate and the species of your tree, you may need to move your bonsai to a sheltered location or provide additional insulation.

Caring for your bonsai through the seasons requires attention, understanding, and patience. By aligning your care practices with your tree's natural cycles, you can support its health and beauty throughout the year. With this seasonal care guide, you'll be well-equipped to meet your bonsai's needs in each season and watch it thrive.

Chapter 13: Pest and Disease Management

Maintaining the health of your bonsai involves vigilance and timely intervention to prevent and treat common pests and diseases. Understanding the signs of these problems and knowing how to address them is essential for preserving your bonsai's vitality. In this chapter, we'll delve into pest and disease management for your bonsai tree.

1. Common Pests in Bonsai

A variety of pests can infest bonsai trees. These include aphids, spider mites, scale insects, and mealybugs, among others. These pests can cause various symptoms, including yellowing leaves, wilting, and decreased vigor.

- **Identification:** Regularly inspect your tree for signs of pests. Look for small insects, discoloration, or sticky residue on the leaves or surrounding surfaces.

- **Prevention:** Maintain a healthy tree, as pests are more likely to infest stressed or weak trees. Regular cleaning of the leaves and surrounding area can also help deter pests.

- **Treatment:** Insecticidal soaps or sprays can be effective against many common pests. In severe cases, a systemic insecticide may be necessary.

2. Common Diseases in Bonsai

Diseases can also affect bonsai trees, including fungal, bacterial, and viral diseases. These can cause symptoms such as spots on leaves, wilting, or even death of parts of the tree.

- **Identification:** Regularly inspect your tree for signs of disease. This may include discolored or spotted leaves, unusual growths, or a general decline in the tree's health.

- **Prevention:** Keep your tree healthy to improve its resistance to disease. Avoid creating conditions that favor disease, such as overly wet or humid conditions.

- **Treatment:** Treatment depends on the specific disease. Fungicides can treat many fungal diseases, while bacterial and viral diseases are more difficult to treat. In some cases, removing the affected parts of the tree may be necessary.

3. Root Rot

Root rot is a common issue, often caused by overwatering or poor drainage. The roots become waterlogged and begin to decay, which can eventually kill the tree.

- **Identification:** Signs of root rot include yellowing or wilting leaves, a foul smell from the soil, or visibly decayed roots when repotting.

- **Prevention:** Ensure your tree is planted in well-draining soil, and avoid overwatering.

- **Treatment:** If caught early, repotting the tree in fresh, well-draining soil and reducing watering can help. Severely decayed roots may need to be pruned.

4. The Role of Quarantine

When introducing a new tree to your collection, it's advisable to quarantine it for a period. This means keeping it separate from your other trees to prevent the potential spread of pests or diseases.

Maintaining the health of your bonsai involves more than just proper watering, feeding, and pruning. Understanding pests and diseases, knowing how to prevent them, and being prepared to treat them promptly are all crucial aspects of bonsai care. By taking these steps, you can keep your bonsai tree vibrant and healthy for many years to come. In the next chapter, we will delve into bonsai display and how best to showcase your miniature masterpiece.

Part V: Advanced Bonsai Techniques

Chapter 14: Advanced Pruning Techniques for Bonsai

Pruning is an essential part of bonsai cultivation. It not only helps maintain the tree's miniature size but also contributes to its artistic shape. While we've discussed basic pruning in earlier chapters, this chapter will delve deeper into advanced techniques that can bring out the full potential of your bonsai tree.

1. Directional Pruning

This technique involves pruning a branch back to a bud or smaller branch that's facing the direction you want the new growth to take. It's an effective way of influencing the future growth of your tree and is particularly useful when you want to give your bonsai a particular shape or style.

2. Defoliation

Defoliation is a more advanced technique that involves removing all the leaves of a tree during the growing season. This encourages the tree to produce a new set of smaller leaves, resulting in a more proportional appearance. This technique should be used carefully, as it places stress on the tree.

3. Pruning to Promote Back Budding

Back budding refers to the development of new buds on older wood, closer to the trunk. Pruning techniques can encourage back budding, which can help you develop a fuller, denser canopy. This includes cutting back to a few leaves on each branch during the growing season.

4. Pruning Conifers

Coniferous trees require specific pruning techniques, such as pinching and candle cutting. Pinching involves removing new growth by hand, while candle cutting refers to cutting off the new growth, or 'candle', that appears in spring.

5. Aesthetic Pruning

Aesthetic pruning is all about enhancing the visual balance and style of your bonsai. This may involve removing branches that disrupt the tree's balance, creating jin and shari to mimic age and weathering, or selectively pruning to highlight certain features.

6. Restorative Pruning

Restorative pruning is used when a tree has become overgrown or its shape has been lost. This involves more drastic cuts to reduce the size of the tree and restore its style. Restorative pruning should be done gradually over time to avoid placing too much stress on the tree.

7. Seasonal Pruning Considerations

The timing of pruning can have a significant impact on how your tree responds. Understanding the best times to perform different types of pruning is crucial. For example, structural pruning is often best done in late winter or early spring, while aesthetic pruning can be done throughout the growing season.

8. Leaf Pruning

Leaf pruning is a technique that can help to reduce leaf size over time, and is especially useful for deciduous trees. It involves removing leaves at their base, leaving the leaf stem attached. This method is usually performed in early summer, and should not be used on weak trees as it can stress the tree significantly.

9. Hardwood Pruning

Hardwood pruning, or structural pruning, focuses on the main branches and trunk of the tree. It is used to shape the tree's overall form and is often performed in late winter when the tree is dormant. This is the time when it's easier to see the tree's structure without the foliage, and the wounds from pruning will heal quickly with the arrival of spring growth.

10. Root Pruning

Root pruning is another advanced technique that's essential in bonsai cultivation. This process helps maintain the tree's miniature size by limiting its resources for growth. It's typically done when repotting the tree, usually every 2-3 years. Care should be taken to ensure a balance between the foliage and roots is maintained to keep the tree healthy.

11. The Role of Wiring in Pruning

While not a form of pruning, wiring is an important technique that's often used in conjunction with pruning. By applying wire to the branches, you can manipulate their direction and shape. Once the tree adapts to this new shape, the wire is removed, and further shaping can be achieved through pruning.

12. Pruning for Health

In addition to aesthetic purposes, pruning is also vital for the health of your bonsai. Removing dead or diseased wood can prevent disease spread. Thinning the canopy can improve air circulation and light penetration, reducing the risk of fungal diseases.

Advanced pruning techniques can truly elevate your bonsai artistry, allowing you to create more complex styles and enhance your tree's aesthetic appeal. However, remember that each cut has a lasting impact on your tree. Always prune with a clear intention and a careful hand. In the next chapter, we will explore how to display your bonsai to best showcase your hard work and your tree's unique beauty.

Chapter 15: Advanced Wiring and Shaping Techniques

Shaping is integral to bonsai cultivation, helping to create the impression of a mature, naturally weathered tree in miniature form. Wiring is one of the most commonly used techniques for shaping bonsai. In this chapter, we'll delve into advanced wiring and shaping techniques that can help you shape your bonsai with precision and artistry.

1. Double-Wiring

Double-wiring involves applying two wires at the same time to manipulate the position of branches or trunks. This technique provides better control over the movement of the branches, allowing for more complex shapes. It's crucial to apply the wires carefully to avoid damaging the bark.

2. Guy-Wiring

Guy-wiring is a method used to bend heavier branches or trunks that can't be shaped with traditional wiring. It involves using a wire attached to the branch and anchored to a more sturdy part of the tree or to the pot. This technique should be used with caution to avoid damaging the tree.

3. Wrap Wiring

Wrap wiring involves wrapping the wire around the branch in a coiled manner. This method is typically used for branches and provides excellent control. However, the wire must be applied at an appropriate angle to avoid damaging the tree and to ensure the branch is held securely.

4. Deadwood Techniques: Jin and Shari

Creating jin (stripped branches) and shari (stripped trunk) can give your bonsai an aged, weather-beaten appearance. These techniques involve stripping the bark from a branch or portion of the trunk to create the look of deadwood.

5. Bending Thick Branches

Bending thicker branches can be challenging. Techniques such as split-branch bending, where the branch is carefully split along its length, or the use of heavy-duty wire, can assist in shaping thicker branches. These techniques require care to prevent irreparable damage to the tree.

6. Using Raffia

Raffia is a type of palm fiber that can be wrapped around a branch to protect it during extreme bending. It helps prevent the branch from cracking or splitting. After soaking raffia in water to make it pliable, it is tightly wound around the branch before applying wire.

7. Maintenance and Care After Wiring

Once wired, the tree needs careful monitoring to ensure the wires don't dig into the growing branches, causing scars. Regular adjustments and eventual removal of the wire are part of the process. It's also important to remember that the tree may require additional water and nutrients due to the stress caused by wiring.

8. The Art of Layering

Layering is an advanced technique that can be used to create new roots from a branch or trunk. The method involves removing a small ring of bark from the area where you want new roots to form and then applying a rooting hormone. The area is then wrapped in sphagnum moss and plastic to maintain humidity. After a few months, roots should form at the site, and the new tree can be separated from the parent plant.

9. Directional Wiring

Directional wiring is used when a particular direction of growth is desired. The wire is applied to the branch in a way that guides the branch in a specific direction. This technique can be especially useful when shaping your bonsai to a specific style.

10. Tourniquet Method

The tourniquet method is another advanced technique used to create new roots. A wire is tightly wrapped around the trunk or branch where you want the roots to develop. Over time, the wire impedes the flow of nutrients, and the tree responds by generating new roots above the wire.

11. Understanding the Influence of Growth Habits

It's essential to understand that every species has unique growth habits and responses to wiring and shaping. Knowing the specific characteristics of your bonsai species can help guide your techniques and expectations. For example, some trees have very flexible branches, while others might be brittle.

12. Styling Old and Mature Bonsai

Working with older, more mature bonsai can be both challenging and rewarding. These trees often require more careful and subtle wiring and shaping techniques to maintain their health and enhance their natural beauty. Always remember to approach mature bonsai with respect and patience, understanding that significant changes can take time.

13.Seasonal Considerations for Wiring and Shaping

Different species of bonsai have different optimal times for wiring and shaping. For many, the best time is during their period of active growth, as the branches are more flexible and the tree can recover more quickly. Always consider the specific needs and characteristics of your tree when planning your wiring and shaping.

Mastering advanced wiring and shaping techniques allows you to create a wide range of styles and forms with your bonsai. These methods require practice, patience, and a gentle hand, but with time, you can use these techniques to bring your vision to life, creating a beautiful, living work of art. In the final chapter, we will discuss how to display your bonsai to showcase its unique beauty and the care you've put into its cultivation.

Chapter 16: Grafting Techniques for Bonsai

Grafting is an advanced skill that can be a valuable tool for the bonsai artist. It allows you to add new branches, change leaf types, or even merge two trees together. This chapter will explore various grafting techniques and provide you with a guide on how to successfully perform these on your bonsai.

1. Approach Grafting

Approach grafting is a technique often used to add a branch to a specific area of the tree. In this process, a small slit is made in the bark of the tree, and a branch (often from the same tree) is inserted into the slit. The branch remains attached to its original location on the tree and continues to receive nutrients as the graft heals.

2. Thread Grafting

Thread grafting is similar to approach grafting, but in this case, a hole is drilled through the trunk or branch of the bonsai. A young shoot from the same tree is then threaded through this hole. Over time, the shoot will graft to its new location, and the original attachment can be severed.

3. Veneer Grafting

Veneer grafting is often used to change the variety of a tree or to repair damage. A veneer (a thin slice of wood with a bud) is taken from one tree and attached to the exposed wood of another tree. Over time, the bud will grow and can eventually replace the original foliage.

4. Whip and Tongue Grafting

Whip and tongue grafting is a more complex technique typically used for creating a new tree or top working an existing tree. Both the scion (the graft) and the rootstock are cut in a way that they can be locked together like puzzle pieces. This technique creates a strong bond and has a high success rate, but it requires precise cuts.

5. Bud Grafting

Bud grafting involves grafting a single bud onto the rootstock. This method is often used to propagate new trees or add a new variety to an existing tree.

6. Aftercare for Grafted Bonsai

Regardless of the grafting technique used, aftercare is critical to ensure the success of the graft. The grafted area should be kept clean, and the tree should be watered and fed regularly. It's also important to provide the tree with a suitable environment for recovery, typically a humid and shaded location.

7. The Art of Bonsai Grafting

Grafting is not just a science; it's also an art. The goal is not just to get the graft to take, but also to do it in a way that enhances the aesthetic appeal of the bonsai.

8. Common Challenges in Bonsai Grafting

Grafting bonsai trees can come with its own set of challenges. Ensuring compatibility between the graft and rootstock, making precise cuts, managing aftercare—these are all critical elements that need careful attention.

9. Root Grafting

Root grafting is a technique used to improve or change the root structure of a bonsai tree. This can be particularly useful if the tree has been damaged or if the roots are not aesthetically pleasing. In this process, a young seedling or cutting is attached to the base of the tree, typically in a similar manner to approach grafting. Over time, the seedling's root system becomes integrated with the tree.

10. Bark Grafting

Bark grafting is another useful method, particularly for larger bonsai. This technique involves inserting the scion between the bark and the wood of the rootstock. The advantage of this method is that it allows for the grafting of larger scions, which can speed up the process of creating new branches or changing the leaf type.

11.Cleft Grafting

Cleft grafting is often used when the rootstock is significantly larger than the scion. A vertical cut is made into the rootstock, and the wedge-shaped scion is inserted into this cleft. This technique can be used to add new branches or to create a new top for a bonsai.

12.Grafting Tools and Equipment

Having the right tools can make a significant difference in grafting success. Sharp knives or grafting tools are essential for making clean cuts that will heal well. It's also beneficial to have grafting tape or wax on hand to protect the graft and encourage healing.

13.Grafting for Reproduction

One of the most exciting applications of grafting is the ability to reproduce your bonsai. If you have a particular tree that you admire, grafting allows you to create a new tree that shares the same characteristics. This can be a rewarding way to expand your bonsai collection or to share your favorite trees with others.

14. Grafting Safety

Finally, it's crucial to remember that grafting involves the use of sharp tools and careful handling of the tree. Always prioritize safety, both for you and the tree. This includes using clean tools to minimize the risk of transmitting diseases and handling the tree gently to avoid causing unnecessary stress or damage.

Grafting is an exciting aspect of bonsai cultivation that opens up new possibilities for your trees. It allows you to manipulate your bonsai in ways that pruning and wiring cannot achieve. As with all bonsai techniques, grafting requires patience, practice, and a gentle hand. In the next chapter, we will discuss how to display your bonsai to highlight its best features and the care and creativity you've put into it.

Part VI: Displaying Your Bonsai

Chapter 17: The Art of Displaying Bonsai

Now that you have painstakingly nurtured your bonsai and mastered various techniques to shape and care for it, it's time to display your living work of art. The way you present your bonsai can dramatically affect the overall perception of its beauty and design. In this chapter, we'll delve into the art of displaying bonsai, helping you showcase your bonsai in the best possible way.

1. Understanding the Basics of Bonsai Display

Displaying bonsai is an art in itself. It requires consideration of the tree's natural form, its environment, and the pot it's housed in. You also need to consider the viewing angle, as it can change the perspective of your bonsai significantly. Finally, think about the backdrop, which should complement and not distract from your bonsai.

2. The Bonsai Pot: Choosing the Right Vessel

The pot is an essential component of the overall bonsai display. It should harmonize with the tree, both in terms of size and style. When selecting a pot, consider its color, shape, and size. It should complement the tree and not draw attention away from it.

3. Bonsai Display Stands

Bonsai display stands add height and prominence to your bonsai. The stand should match the style of the tree and the pot. Traditional bonsai stands have a minimalist design, often crafted from bamboo or wood. The stand should be sturdy and able to support the weight of the bonsai.

4. The Display Area: Considering Space and Light

The display area should provide a tranquil setting for your bonsai. Natural light is critical, but avoid areas with direct sunlight that can scorch the leaves. Ambient temperature should also be considered, depending on the bonsai species. If displaying indoors, ensure the space isn't prone to sudden temperature changes.

5. Bonsai Companions: Accentuating with Companion Plants and Objects

Companion plants, rocks, and other objects can be used to enhance your bonsai display. These items, often called "shitakusa," create a miniature landscape around your bonsai, adding to the story and visual interest. These elements should complement but not overwhelm your bonsai.

6. Seasonal Displays

Bonsai displays can be altered to reflect the changing seasons. Seasonal adjustments can include changing companion plants, altering the display backdrop, or even rotating different bonsai into the display area based on their season of peak interest.

7. The Art of Tokonoma Display

A traditional Japanese method of displaying bonsai is in a "tokonoma," an alcove specifically designed for artistic display. This setup often includes a hanging scroll, an accent piece, and the bonsai itself. Each element is carefully chosen to reflect the season and create a harmonious composition.

8. Public Displays and Exhibitions

If you choose to exhibit your bonsai in public, there are additional considerations, such as transporting your bonsai safely, adhering to exhibition display rules, and preparing your bonsai to look its best on the day of the exhibition.

9. Photographing Your Bonsai

Capturing the beauty of your bonsai through photography is another form of display. It allows you to share your bonsai with others and keep a visual record of your bonsai's development over time. Good photography considers the lighting, composition, and focus to best showcase your bonsai.

10. Outdoor Bonsai Display

Outdoor display spaces open up more possibilities for your bonsai. You can create larger display areas, incorporate elements of the surrounding landscape, and provide a more natural environment for your bonsai. Be aware of the climate, potential pests, and ensure the bonsai are species suitable for your outdoor conditions.

11. Viewing Angles and Perspective

It's essential to consider how your bonsai will be viewed. From above, at eye level, or from below? Each perspective provides a unique view. For most displays, bonsai are best viewed at eye level to appreciate the full structure and design of the tree.

12. Displaying Bonsai Groups

Displaying a group of bonsai, or a "yose-ue," presents a unique challenge. Each tree in the group should contribute to the overall design, but one usually acts as the focal point. The arrangement of the trees should suggest a natural landscape, with each tree interacting harmoniously with others in the group.

13. Displaying Bonsai Forests

A bonsai forest, or "ikadabuki," is another display style, where multiple trees of the same species are planted together to form a miniature forest. This type of display emphasizes the trees' scale and interplay, creating a sense of depth and perspective.

14. Traditional vs. Modern Bonsai Display

While traditional bonsai display rules provide a useful guide, modern displays often take a more flexible approach. Contemporary displays may experiment with different styles of pots, stands, and companion pieces, and use unconventional display spaces.

15. Caring for Your Bonsai Display

A bonsai display requires regular care, just like the trees themselves. Regular cleaning of the display area, the stand, the pot, and any display companions is necessary. Regularly check the health of your bonsai and ensure the display conditions continue to meet its needs.

16. Honoring the Bonsai Aesthetic

The purpose of displaying bonsai is to showcase their beauty and the skill involved in their creation. Every element of the display should serve to highlight the bonsai and create a sense of harmony and tranquility.

Displaying your bonsai is the final step in the bonsai cultivation journey, but it's a step that requires careful thought and planning. The display is your opportunity to showcase your bonsai's beauty and the effort you've put into shaping and caring for it. Whether it's for your own personal.

Chapter 18: Indoor vs. Outdoor Display: What You Need to Know

As you delve into the art of bonsai, one fundamental question you'll need to answer is where you'll be displaying your bonsai - indoors or outdoors? The location of your bonsai can significantly influence its growth, health, and overall appearance. This chapter will guide you through the essential factors to consider when deciding between an indoor and outdoor display.

- **Understanding the Natural Habitat of Your Bonsai**

The first step is understanding the natural environment of your specific bonsai species. Some trees are suited to a temperate climate and require the changing seasons to thrive, while others are tropical or subtropical and can flourish indoors with consistent conditions. Understanding your bonsai's needs will help you make the best decision for its location.

- **Indoor Bonsai Display: Benefits and Challenges**

Indoor displays allow you to enjoy your bonsai year-round in a controlled environment. You can protect your bonsai from harsh weather conditions, pests, and diseases more effectively. However, it can be challenging to provide adequate sunlight indoors, and the lack of seasonal changes can be detrimental to certain species. Additionally, maintaining the right humidity levels can be a challenge inside homes where air conditioning or heating is used.

- **Outdoor Bonsai Display: Benefits and Challenges**

  Outdoor displays align more closely with the natural habitat of many bonsai species. They allow for exposure to sunlight, air circulation, and seasonal changes, which many trees require for healthy growth. On the downside, outdoor bonsai are susceptible to severe weather conditions, pests, and diseases. You also need to consider security for your bonsai when displayed outside.

- **Transitioning Bonsai between Indoors and Outdoors**

  Some bonsai enthusiasts choose to move their trees in and out, depending on the season. This method can offer the best of both worlds but requires careful monitoring of weather conditions and a gradual transition to avoid shocking the tree.

- **Light Requirements**

  Light is crucial for photosynthesis, the process by which plants feed themselves. Outdoors, your bonsai will generally receive ample light. Indoors, however, you may need to supplement natural light with grow lights, especially in winter months or darker rooms.

- **Temperature and Humidity Considerations**

  Outdoor bonsai will experience natural seasonal changes, which can encourage dormancy in temperate species. Indoor bonsai, on the other hand, are exposed to a more consistent climate. Humidity trays or humidifiers may be necessary to supplement humidity levels indoors.

- **Display Aesthetics**

  Indoor and outdoor displays can each offer unique aesthetic appeal. Indoors, your bonsai can become an integral part of your interior design. Outdoors, your bonsai can enhance your garden landscape and offer a more natural setting.

- **Bonsai Maintenance: Indoor vs. Outdoor**

  Both indoor and outdoor bonsai require diligent care, but the maintenance tasks may differ. Watering, fertilizing, pruning, and repotting must be adapted to the environment and the specific needs of your bonsai.

- **Best Trees for Indoor and Outdoor Display**

  Not all trees are suited for both indoor and outdoor display. Species such as Ficus, Jade, and Sago Palm can be successful indoors, while

Japanese Maple, Juniper, and Pine often fare better outdoors.

- **Space Requirements**

    Bonsai do not require a vast amount of space, but it's essential to ensure they have room to grow and are not overcrowded. Outdoor bonsai may have more room to spread out, while indoor bonsai may need to be rotated to ensure they receive even light exposure.

- **Specialized Bonsai Displays**

    For dedicated bonsai enthusiasts, constructing a specialized display area can enhance your bonsai's aesthetic appeal. Outdoors, this could be a designated area in your garden, a bonsai bench, or even a full bonsai pavilion. Indoors, it could be a custom display shelf or an alcove in your living room.

- **Impact of Display Location on Bonsai Health**

    The display location can impact your bonsai's health significantly. An indoor bonsai may suffer if placed near a heat vent or in a drafty area. Outdoors, your bonsai could be damaged by strong winds, heavy rain, or intense sun. Choosing the best location for your bonsai's health is paramount.

- **The Influence of Display Orientation**

The direction your bonsai faces can also affect its growth. Bonsai placed near a window indoors may grow towards the light, requiring regular rotation. Outdoor bonsai in the northern hemisphere will get more sun if facing south, which can impact its watering needs.

- **Considerations for Multiple Bonsai**

If you have more than one bonsai, you'll need to consider how they interact. Each bonsai should have its space to grow, and more dominant trees should not overshadow smaller or less assertive species.

- **Accessibility for Care**

Regardless of whether your bonsai are indoors or outdoors, ensure that they are easily accessible for care. Watering, pruning, and other maintenance tasks will be much easier if you can easily reach all sides of your bonsai.

- **Creating an Immersive Bonsai Experience**

Some bonsai enthusiasts go beyond a simple display and create an entire bonsai experience, complete with paths to walk, benches to sit and contemplate, and various display areas to explore. This can be done either indoors, with sufficient space, or outdoors.

Understanding the pros and cons of indoor and outdoor bonsai display can help you make an informed decision on where to place your bonsai. Whichever location you choose, remember that careful monitoring and regular care are crucial to keeping your bonsai healthy and beautiful. In the next chapter, we will discuss how to continue your bonsai education and explore other advanced techniques.

Chapter 19: Bonsai and Feng Shui: Harmonizing Your Space

Feng Shui, an ancient Chinese philosophy, focuses on balancing energies in a given space to promote health, prosperity, and overall well-being. Incorporating a bonsai tree into your space with Feng Shui principles can create a harmonious environment. This chapter will guide you through integrating your bonsai display with the principles of Feng Shui.

- **Understanding Feng Shui**

Feng Shui is about organizing your surroundings to establish harmony and balance. It's guided by the Taoist vision and understanding of nature, particularly on the idea that the land is alive and filled with Chi, or energy. In the context of bonsai, Feng Shui can help place your bonsai to best harmonize with your environment.

- **The Five Elements in Feng Shui**

In Feng Shui, there are five elements - Wood, Fire, Earth, Metal, and Water. Each element interacts with the others in productive and destructive cycles. A bonsai, representing the Wood element, can be used to strengthen or soften the presence of these elements in your space depending on its placement.

- **The Bagua Map**

    The Bagua is the Feng Shui energy map of your space. The Bagua divides any given space into eight areas or 'guas,' each corresponding to different life aspects, such as wealth, health, and career. Placing your bonsai in the appropriate gua can enhance that area's energy.

- **Placement of Your Bonsai Tree**

    Proper placement of your bonsai is critical in Feng Shui. For instance, placing your bonsai in the East sector of your home (Family & Health area) can promote health and strong relationships, as this area is related to the Wood element. However, avoid placing the bonsai in the bedroom, as active energy from plants can disturb rest.

- **Bonsai Shape and Feng Shui**

    The shape of your bonsai can also influence its Feng Shui energy. Upright shapes promote growth and upward movement, while cascading shapes can inspire tranquility and inward reflection. Choosing a shape that aligns with your intentions can enhance your bonsai's influence.

- **Bonsai Species and Feng Shui**

    Different species of bonsai can carry different Feng Shui meanings. For example, the Pine symbolizes endurance and longevity, while the

Cherry Blossom represents new beginnings and the transience of life.

- **Color in Bonsai and Feng Shui**

    Color plays a vital role in Feng Shui as each color corresponds to a specific Feng Shui element. Green bonsai promotes healing and balance, while red or pink blooms can inspire love and passion.

- **Incorporating Water Elements**

    Water is one of the five essential elements in Feng Shui. Incorporating a water feature, like a small pond or fountain near your bonsai, can enhance the flow of positive energy or Chi.

- **Caring for Your Bonsai: A Feng Shui Perspective**

    Just like any living element in Feng Shui, your bonsai requires care and attention. Neglected or unhealthy bonsai can create negative energy. Regular care, on the other hand, not only helps your bonsai thrive but also promotes positive Chi.

- **Creating Balance with Bonsai**

    Balance is the core of Feng Shui. A well-balanced bonsai, harmoniously combining its shape, size, color, pot, and placement, can significantly contribute to achieving the desired balance in your space.

- **Understanding Yin and Yang in Bonsai Display**

Yin and Yang represent the duality of nature according to Chinese philosophy. In terms of bonsai, a tree can have aspects of both: the robust, sturdy trunk (Yang), and the delicate, flowing branches and foliage (Yin). Balancing these elements in your bonsai can also contribute to balanced chi.

- **The Significance of Numbers**

In Feng Shui, numbers hold significant meanings. Odd numbers, especially the number 9, are considered particularly auspicious. You might consider displaying your bonsai in groups of three or five, or trimming your bonsai to have nine main branches.

- **Directions and Bonsai**

The direction your bonsai faces or leans can also impact the energy of your space. A tree leaning towards the left (when looking at it) can activate Yin energy, which is calming and restorative. Conversely, a tree leaning to the right can stimulate more active, vibrant Yang energy.

- **The Role of Bonsai Pots in Feng Shui**

The pot is also an essential part of your bonsai display. The color, shape, and material of your bonsai pot can either enhance or counteract certain energies. For instance, a red or orange pot can stimulate Fire energy, while a round or oval pot can promote a more harmonious, balanced energy.

- **Enhancing Personal Areas of the Bagua with Bonsai**

Bonsai can be used to energize specific areas of your life according to the Bagua. If you wish to stimulate wealth and prosperity, placing a healthy, flourishing bonsai in the southeast area of your home can help to manifest this.

- **Bonsai and Feng Shui in the Garden**

If you display your bonsai outdoors, you can apply the principles of garden Feng Shui. Your bonsai can be used to create a balanced, peaceful sanctuary, harmonizing with other elements such as water features, rocks, and other plants.

- **The Effect of Seasons on Bonsai and Feng Shui**

The changing seasons can influence the energy of your bonsai. Spring and summer, with vibrant growth and blossoming flowers, can activate Yang energy. In contrast, autumn and winter, with falling leaves and a period of dormancy, can stimulate more introspective, Yin energy.

By mindfully incorporating your bonsai into your space with Feng Shui principles, you can create a peaceful, harmonious environment that not only highlights the beauty of your bonsai but also promotes positive energy flow and well-being. In the next chapter, we will explore the art of bonsai display and presentation, focusing on aesthetic principles and traditional display conventions.

Part VII: Long-lasting Bonsai

Chapter 20: Ensuring the Longevity of Your Bonsai

A well-cared bonsai tree can outlive its caretaker, becoming a living heirloom passed down through generations. Ensuring the longevity of your bonsai involves ongoing, careful maintenance and a deep understanding of your tree's needs. This chapter will provide valuable insights and tips to help your bonsai thrive for many years.

1. Recognizing Your Bonsai's Lifespan

Different species of bonsai have different expected lifespans. Some trees, like junipers or pines, can live for hundreds of years, while others may only last a few decades. Understanding your tree's natural lifespan can help set realistic expectations for its longevity.

2. Proper Watering Practices

Proper watering is fundamental to the survival and longevity of your bonsai. Both overwatering and underwatering can severely damage your tree. Understanding the water needs of your particular bonsai species is critical to its long-term health.

3. Balanced Fertilization

Providing your bonsai with the necessary nutrients is another key to its longevity. However, remember that too much of a good thing can be harmful. Over-fertilizing can lead to nutrient burn and other problems. Use a balanced bonsai-specific fertilizer and follow the recommended application schedule.

4. Regular Pruning and Trimming

Regular pruning and trimming help maintain your bonsai's shape and health. Pruning encourages new growth, helps to maintain the tree's size and shape, and allows for better air circulation and light penetration.

5. Seasonal Care

Your bonsai's care needs will change with the seasons. In the spring and summer, your tree will need more frequent watering and fertilization. In the fall and winter, your bonsai will enter a dormant period where it requires less care.

6. Pest and Disease Management

Pests and diseases can significantly shorten your bonsai's lifespan if not promptly addressed. Regular inspections of your bonsai will help you spot and treat any issues early on, preventing further damage.

7. Proper Repotting Practices

Repotting is a crucial aspect of bonsai care that promotes the health and longevity of your tree. As a rule, bonsai should be repotted every two to five years, depending on the species and its growth rate.

8. Environmental Considerations

The environment in which your bonsai lives can have a significant impact on its longevity. Bonsai trees need a certain amount of light, suitable temperature ranges, and proper humidity levels to thrive.

9. Preventing Common Bonsai Mistakes

Some common mistakes can jeopardize the longevity of your bonsai. These include overwatering, incorrect placement (too much or too little light), and neglecting seasonal care needs.

10. Creating a Care Schedule

Creating a care schedule can help ensure that you don't miss any critical care steps. This schedule can include watering, fertilizing, pruning, and other tasks, depending on your bonsai's specific needs.

11. Advanced Techniques for Longevity

Some advanced techniques can also contribute to your bonsai's longevity. These may include air-layering (to rejuvenate old bonsai), grafting (to add vitality or improve the form), and creating jin and shari (to enhance the aged appearance of the tree).

12. The Role of Patience and Observation

Lastly, cultivating patience and keen observation skills is integral to ensuring your bonsai's longevity. Noticing subtle changes in your bonsai's appearance can provide early indications of potential issues.

13. Understanding Your Bonsai's Dormancy Cycle

Most bonsai trees, especially those from temperate climates, have a dormancy cycle. Understanding this cycle is crucial to your bonsai's health. Providing a period of rest during the colder months, mirroring the tree's natural environment, can help promote its longevity.

14. Avoiding Root Bound Conditions

A bonsai can become root-bound if it has been too long in the same pot. The roots can fill the pot entirely, leaving no room for new growth. Regular repotting not only replenishes the soil's nutrients but also prevents the tree from becoming root-bound.

15. Adequate Sunlight and Proper Placement

Proper placement of your bonsai is key to its survival. All trees need light for photosynthesis, so make sure your bonsai gets plenty of indirect, but bright light. Rotate your tree every few days to ensure all parts receive light and grow evenly.

16. Protection from Extreme Conditions

Protecting your bonsai from extreme conditions is critical to its longevity. Whether it's a heatwave, a deep freeze, or a storm, ensuring your bonsai is protected can prevent damage and stress that could impact its lifespan.

17. The Importance of Cleanliness

Keeping your bonsai and its surrounding area clean helps prevent the spread of diseases and pests. This includes cleaning your tools between uses, removing any fallen debris from the tree and its pot, and keeping the foliage clean.

18. Regular Health Checks

Regular health checks help catch potential problems before they escalate. Look for signs of pests or disease, such as changes in leaf color, spots, or the presence of insects. Regularly inspect the trunk, branches, leaves, and roots for any signs of decay or damage.

19.Adapting Care to Your Tree's Age

As your bonsai ages, its needs will change. Older trees typically grow slower, requiring less frequent pruning and feeding. Their watering needs might also change. Being adaptable and responsive to your tree's changing needs can contribute significantly to its longevity.

20.Learning from Mistakes

Even the most experienced bonsai practitioners make mistakes. The key is to learn from these mistakes rather than be disheartened by them. Each error is an opportunity to better understand your tree and improve its care.

21.Cultivating a Relationship with Your Bonsai

Developing a deep connection with your bonsai can also contribute to its longevity. When you're emotionally invested in your bonsai, you're more likely to provide it with the attentive care it needs. View your bonsai not just as a plant, but as a companion.

Ensuring the longevity of your bonsai tree is a long-term commitment, requiring time, care, and attention. But the reward is a beautiful, living piece of art that provides serenity. Bonsai cultivation is a journey. Each tree is unique, and understanding its individual needs and characteristics is part of the pleasure and challenge. With the right care and attention, your bonsai can provide beauty and enjoyment for generations to come. In the next chapter, we'll explore how to propagate bonsai trees, so you can expand your collection and share the joy of bonsai with others.

Chapter 21: Bonsai through the Seasons: Year-round Care

The practice of bonsai cultivation isn't a seasonal hobby; it's a year-round commitment. While the needs of your bonsai change with the seasons, they always require attention and care. This chapter outlines the yearly cycle of bonsai care to ensure their health and longevity.

1. Understanding Seasonal Changes

Firstly, understanding how each season impacts the growth and dormancy of your bonsai tree is crucial. The length of daylight, temperature fluctuations, and changes in humidity all influence your bonsai's biological processes.

2. Spring Care: Awakening from Dormancy

In spring, your bonsai begins to awaken from its winter dormancy. This is the time for repotting, heavy pruning, and fertilizing. It's also essential to keep a close eye on water requirements as new growth uses up more water.

3. Early Summer Care: Growth and Shaping

Early summer is the period of most vigorous growth for your bonsai. The focus during this season is on shaping the new growth using wiring and pruning techniques. Regular watering is crucial during this period due to increased temperatures.

4. Mid to Late Summer Care: Maintenance and Health

During mid to late summer, maintenance is key. The vigorous growth of early summer slows, and it's an excellent time to ensure the tree's overall health. Pests and diseases are more common in summer, so regular inspections are important.

5. Fall Care: Preparation for Dormancy

As temperatures drop and daylight hours decrease in fall, your bonsai prepares for dormancy. It's the time to gradually reduce watering and halt fertilization to allow the tree to slow its growth. Removing any dead leaves or needles will help prevent potential pest problems.

6. Winter Care: Dormancy and Protection

During winter, your bonsai enters a period of dormancy. While watering needs are reduced significantly, the tree should not be allowed to dry out completely. Protecting your tree from extreme winter conditions is crucial. Some trees may need to be moved indoors or into a cold frame to protect them from harsh weather.

7. Special Considerations for Tropical Bonsai

Tropical and subtropical bonsai varieties require special consideration, as they don't have a dormancy period like temperate species. These trees need consistent care throughout the year, with a focus on maintaining a warm and humid environment, especially in winter.

8. Seasonal Fertilization Schedule

Understanding the different nutrient requirements of your bonsai throughout the seasons is crucial. Spring and early summer are times of vigorous growth and therefore need more nutrient supplementation. In contrast, fertilizer application should be reduced or stopped altogether in late fall and winter.

9. Seasonal Repotting Considerations

Repotting is typically done in the spring when your tree has the whole growing season to recover. However, some trees may benefit from fall repotting. Always consider the specific needs of your tree.

10. Adjusting Bonsai Positioning with Seasons

The amount of light and heat your bonsai gets should be adjusted with the seasons. In summer, it might be necessary to protect your tree from the scorching midday sun. In contrast, maximizing light exposure is essential during the darker winter months.

11. Managing Pests and Diseases Year-round

Different pests and diseases can appear in different seasons. A regular year-round inspection schedule can catch problems early, preventing significant damage.

12. Understanding Your Bonsai's Natural Habitat

The species of your bonsai tree determines its natural habitat, which in turn, affects how it responds to seasonal changes. Understanding the native environment of your tree species will give you valuable insight into its optimal care throughout the year.

13. Recognizing Seasonal Signs in Your Bonsai

Your bonsai tree will give you signs that it is entering a new phase or season. Recognizing these signs, such as new buds in spring or leaf drop in fall, can help you adjust your care routines appropriately.

14. Seasonal Pruning and Wiring

Pruning and wiring practices can also change with the seasons. For instance, heavy pruning is usually done in spring when the tree can recover quickly, while maintenance pruning can be carried out throughout the year. Wiring is typically done when the tree is not in its growth phase to minimize damage.

15.Overwintering Bonsai

Overwintering involves protecting your bonsai from harsh winter conditions. Depending on your tree's species and your local climate, overwintering strategies can vary from using cold frames or greenhouses to bringing your tree indoors.

16.Seasonal Soil Considerations

Different seasons might demand adjustments to your bonsai soil mix. For instance, during rainy seasons, a well-draining soil mix is crucial to prevent waterlogging, while a moisture-retaining mix might be beneficial in hot summers.

17.Adjusting Watering Techniques and Frequency

Watering practices need to be adjusted according to seasonal needs. While summer demands more frequent watering, winter requires reduced watering. The method of watering can also change, with misting being particularly beneficial during hot summers to increase humidity.

18.Seasonal Stress Factors

Each season can bring unique stress factors for your bonsai. Heat stress in summer, cold stress in winter, or even transition stress when moving between seasons. Being aware of these stressors can help you provide preventative care and timely intervention.

19.Incorporating Seasonal Display Elements

For those who like to display their bonsai, incorporating elements that represent the current season can enhance your display's aesthetic and narrative. For instance, a flowering accent plant in spring or a miniature snowman figurine in winter.

20.Engaging with a Bonsai Community

Joining a local bonsai club or online community can provide valuable insights and tips specific to your local climate and the current season. Experienced members can offer advice based on years, if not decades, of bonsai cultivation.

Through dedicated, year-round care, your bonsai tree can not only survive but thrive, reflecting the beauty of each passing season. Up next, we'll be diving into the fascinating process of bonsai propagation. So if you've ever dreamed of expanding your bonsai collection, you'll want to keep reading. With a clear understanding of the yearly cycle of bonsai care, you can ensure your tree thrives in all seasons. Remember, each tree is unique, so it's important to understand and respect its individual needs. In the next chapter, we'll explore the fascinating world of bonsai propagation.

Chapter 22: Repotting Your Bonsai: When and How

Repotting is a critical part of bonsai care. It ensures the health and longevity of your tree by providing it with fresh soil, more room for growth, and the opportunity to manage root health. This chapter will guide you through the whys, whens, and hows of repotting your bonsai tree.

1. The Importance of Repotting

Repotting is more than just changing the soil or the pot. It involves careful root pruning, which stimulates healthier and denser root growth. Additionally, it gives you the opportunity to refresh the nutrient-rich soil, ensuring your bonsai receives the nutrients it needs.

2. Identifying When to Repot

Knowing when to repot your bonsai tree is essential. The frequency varies depending on the species, age, and size of your tree. However, general signs that your bonsai needs repotting include: water not absorbing properly and running off the soil surface, slower growth, and roots appearing on the soil surface or out of the drainage holes.

3. Choosing the Right Time of Year

Typically, repotting is best done in late winter or early spring when the tree is still dormant but about to enter the growing season. This timing allows the tree to recover from the stress of repotting before focusing on new growth.

4. Preparing for Repotting

Before you begin the repotting process, gather all necessary materials: a suitable bonsai pot, fresh bonsai soil mix, a root rake, pruning shears, wire for anchoring, and perhaps a screen for the drainage holes. Also, consider preparing a suitable workspace that can handle a bit of a mess.

5. Removing the Bonsai from its Pot

Carefully remove the bonsai from its pot, ensuring you don't cause undue stress to the tree. You might need to use a root rake or chopstick to gently loosen the soil and roots around the edges of the pot.

6. Root Pruning

Using a root rake, comb out the roots to remove old soil and untangle them. Once detangled, use sharp, clean pruning shears to trim away excess roots. Remember to be conservative; the aim is to promote health, not to damage the tree.

7. Selecting and Preparing the New Pot

The new pot can be the old one (cleaned thoroughly) or a new one that suits your tree's needs. Ensure it has sufficient drainage holes. You may place screens over the holes to prevent soil loss, then add a layer of fresh bonsai soil to the pot.

8. Placing the Tree in the New Pot

Position your tree in the new pot. The best placement depends on the tree's shape and style, but usually, it's not dead center. Once you're happy with the position, you can start adding soil around the roots.

9. Securing the Tree

To prevent your tree from shifting, you'll need to secure it. Run wire up from the bottom of the pot, loop it over the root ball, and tighten gently. Be careful not to damage the trunk or major roots.

10. Final Steps After Repotting

After repotting, water your bonsai thoroughly until water runs out of the drainage holes. This helps the fresh soil settle around the roots. Keep the tree in a shaded, protected area for a few weeks to allow it to recover from repotting stress.

11. Post-repotting Care

After repotting, your tree will need a little extra care. Watering should be monitored closely as the fresh soil will retain water differently. Hold off on fertilizing until you see new growth, indicating that the tree has recovered and is ready to absorb nutrients.

12.Root Care during Repotting

While removing old soil and untangling the roots, be gentle to prevent unnecessary damage. Remember that roots are the lifeline of your bonsai tree and should be treated with care.

13.Root-Over-Rock and Exposed Root Styles

For bonsai trees cultivated in specific styles like root-over-rock or exposed root, repotting requires extra care to maintain the unique root structure. The roots are a central part of these bonsai styles' aesthetics and thus should be preserved and enhanced during repotting.

14.Understanding Soil Composition

Different bonsai trees may require different soil mixes. Understanding your bonsai's specific needs is crucial. Bonsai soils often consist of varying ratios of organic and inorganic components, each with unique benefits for your tree's growth and health.

15.Preparing Your Bonsai Soil Mix

Prepare your bonsai soil mix in advance. This mix should be well-draining to prevent waterlogging and root rot but should also retain enough moisture to keep the tree hydrated. The right soil mix will also support nutrient uptake and allow room for root growth.

16.Selecting the Right Bonsai Pot

Selecting the right pot is not just about size; it's also about style, color, and material. The pot should harmonize with your bonsai tree, complementing its aesthetics without drawing attention away from the tree itself.

17.Upgrading to a Larger Pot

If your tree has outgrown its current pot, you may need to upgrade to a larger one. This gives the roots more room to grow, promoting overall tree health. However, remember that a bonsai's charm lies in its miniature size, so keep the pot proportionate to the tree.

18.Repotting Multi-tree Bonsai

If you have a group planting or forest-style bonsai, repotting can be more complex. You'll need to take care of each tree's roots and ensure that the entire composition remains aesthetically pleasing.

19.Dealing with Old, Hardened Soil

Over time, soil can become compacted and hard, making repotting a challenge. Soaking the root ball in water can help soften hardened soil and make it easier to remove.

20.Repotting Aftercare: Temperature and Light

After repotting, protect your bonsai from extreme temperatures, winds, and direct sunlight. These can stress the tree and impede recovery. Keep it in a sheltered location with gentle, indirect light until new growth appears.

Repotting is a vital procedure in bonsai cultivation. By mastering it, you're one step closer to ensuring your bonsai tree's health and longevity. In the next chapter, we'll explore the artistic aspects of bonsai, delving into the principles of aesthetics and design that make each bonsai unique.

Conclusion

The Journey Ahead: Continuing Your Bonsai Practice

Caring for bonsai is more than just a hobby or an art form—it's a journey of continual learning, patience, and connection with nature. You've embarked on this journey, gaining fundamental knowledge and skills, and as our guidebook draws to a close, let's reflect on the path ahead and how you can deepen your bonsai practice.

1. Building on Bonsai Fundamentals

The information and techniques provided in this guide are just the beginning. With these fundamentals in hand, you can now delve deeper into the world of bonsai, exploring more complex styles, techniques, and species. Remember, learning and improvement come with time and practice.

2. The Value of Patience

One of the most important lessons bonsai cultivation teaches us is patience. Bonsai trees grow slowly, and their care demands regular attention over long periods. Embrace this aspect of the practice, for it is in these quiet moments of care that you connect most profoundly with your bonsai.

3. Cultivating Observation Skills

Bonsai care requires keen observation skills. Noticing subtle changes in your tree's foliage, root system, or growth patterns can be the key to maintaining its health and shaping its form. Continue to hone this skill—the more intimately you know your bonsai, the more effectively you can care for it.

4. Expanding Your Bonsai Collection

As you gain confidence and experience, consider expanding your bonsai collection. Different tree species offer diverse growth habits, leaf shapes, and care requirements, enriching your bonsai experience.

5. Exploring Advanced Techniques

As your bonsai journey progresses, you might wish to explore advanced techniques such as grafting, creating jin and shari (deadwood features), or cultivating group plantings. Each of these techniques opens new avenues of artistic expression and horticultural skill.

6. Joining a Bonsai Community

Whether locally or online, consider joining a bonsai community. Fellow enthusiasts can offer advice, inspiration, and camaraderie. Bonsai exhibitions and workshops are also excellent ways to learn and draw inspiration.

7. Bonsai as a Lifelong Practice

Cultivating bonsai is a lifelong journey of learning and growth. Like the trees you care for, your skills and understanding will deepen over time. With patience, dedication, and a keen eye, you can cultivate not only beautiful bonsai but also a profound appreciation for the beauty and complexity of nature.

8. Sharing the Joy of Bonsai

Bonsai is a joy to be shared. Consider gifting bonsai to friends or family, teaching others about the practice, or exhibiting your trees. Sharing your passion for bonsai can bring others closer to nature and cultivate appreciation for this profound art form.

9. Reflecting on Your Bonsai Journey

Take time to reflect on your bonsai journey— consider keeping a bonsai journal to record your observations, successes, and challenges. Reflection is not just an opportunity to track your progress but also a way to deepen your connection with your bonsai trees.

10.Looking Ahead

As you look to the future, consider the legacy of your bonsai trees. With proper care, your bonsai can outlive you, becoming a living testament to your patience, care, and artistic vision.

11.Honoring the History and Traditions of Bonsai

As you advance in your bonsai journey, take time to learn more about the historical and cultural roots of bonsai. This deep understanding will add another layer of appreciation to your practice and may inform your stylistic choices.

12.Bonsai as a Form of Meditation

Many bonsai practitioners find the care routine – watering, pruning, wiring – meditative. It's a time of stillness and focus. As you continue your bonsai practice, you may find it becomes a welcome retreat from the hustle and bustle of everyday life.

13.Furthering Your Education

There are many resources available to further your bonsai knowledge. Books, online tutorials, and workshops can deepen your understanding of the art and science of bonsai. Never stop learning, as there is always more to discover.

14.Experimentation in Bonsai

While there are guidelines and techniques to follow, don't be afraid to experiment. Each tree is unique and may not fit perfectly into traditional bonsai styles or techniques. Trust your instincts and learn from each experience, successful or not.

15.Respect for Nature

Bonsai is an intimate interaction with nature. It's about respect, harmony, and understanding. As you continue your bonsai journey, this connection with nature will deepen, and you will start to see the natural world with new eyes.

16.Visiting Public Bonsai Collections

Consider visiting public bonsai collections or exhibitions. Seeing other bonsai trees can provide inspiration, new ideas, and an appreciation for the vast possibilities of this art form.

17.Bonsai in All Seasons

A bonsai tree is a living artwork that changes with the seasons. Observe your tree throughout the year, noting how it responds to each season. This understanding can help guide your care routine and artistic decisions.

18.Building Resilience

Bonsai cultivation will have its challenges—pests, diseases, or even a tree that doesn't survive. These experiences, while difficult, are part of the journey. They build resilience, deepen your understanding, and ultimately make you a better bonsai artist.

19.The Reward of Patience

Bonsai cultivation is a slow art. The tree you're shaping today may not reach its full potential for many years. But the reward of patience is great – a mature, beautifully shaped bonsai tree that you've nurtured and guided over time.

20.Passing on Your Knowledge

As you accumulate knowledge and experience, consider passing it on. Whether you teach a friend, a younger family member, or the wider community, sharing your passion for bonsai can enrich others' lives and ensure the future of this timeless art form.

Bonsai cultivation is a rewarding and enriching journey that can span a lifetime. As you step forward on this path, remember that every bonsai tree, like every bonsai artist, is unique. Cultivate your trees with patience and care, and they will reward you with beauty, tranquility, and a deeper connection with the natural world. Enjoy the journey!

Bonsai Species Guide: Profiles of Popular Bonsai Trees

Choosing the right tree species for your bonsai is crucial. Each species has its own growth habits, care needs, and unique characteristics that can influence its suitability for different styles of bonsai. Here are some popular species to consider:

1. Japanese Maple (Acer palmatum)

Japanese Maple is a favorite among bonsai enthusiasts for its vibrant foliage that changes color with the seasons. It's best suited for outdoor cultivation and requires a period of winter dormancy.

2. Chinese Elm (Ulmus parvifolia)

Chinese Elm is adaptable, resilient, and perfect for beginners. Its small leaves, fine branches, and ability to thrive both indoors and outdoors make it a versatile choice.

3. Juniper (Juniperus)

With many species and varieties, Junipers are evergreen conifers popular for their rugged, natural appearance. They're typically outdoor bonsai and do well in a variety of styles, including cascade and windswept.

4. Ficus (Ficus)

Ficus species, like the Ficus Retusa, are excellent for indoor bonsai due to their tolerance to lower light conditions. They're known for their unique root structures and lush, glossy leaves.

5. Pine (Pinus)

Pine trees are classic bonsai subjects, symbolizing endurance and stoicism. The Japanese Black Pine and White Pine are particularly popular. They're outdoor trees that require plenty of sunlight.

6. Azalea (Rhododendron)

Azaleas are prized for their spectacular spring flowers. The Satsuki Azalea variety is commonly used in bonsai for its numerous flower colors and patterns. Azaleas prefer outdoor conditions with good sunlight and a cool winter period.

7. Cypress (Chamaecyparis/Cupressus)

Cypress trees have fine, feathery foliage that can be molded into elegant shapes. They are often seen in formal upright, informal upright, and group planting styles. They are outdoor bonsai that prefer full sun and well-draining soil.

8. Boxwood (Buxus)

Boxwoods are tough, versatile, and beginner-friendly. Their small leaves, dense growth habits, and responsiveness to pruning make them ideal for detailed shaping.

9. Banyan-Style Fig (Ficus benghalensis)

The Banyan-Style Fig is known for its aerial roots that form additional trunks once they reach the soil. This species is best kept outdoors in warmer climates, but it can also do well indoors with sufficient light.

10. Beech (Fagus)

Beech trees have beautiful, smooth bark, and their leaves change color in autumn. The European Beech and Japanese Beech are popular choices. They are outdoor bonsai that require a winter dormancy period.

11. Pomegranate (Punica granatum)

The Pomegranate is an attractive choice for bonsai due to its lovely flowers and fruit. This deciduous shrub prefers full sunlight and can adapt well to dry conditions. It's an outdoor species that benefits from a period of winter dormancy.

12. Crabapple (Malus)

The Crabapple is admired for its spring blossoms and small, colorful autumn fruits. It's best suited to temperate outdoor climates and requires a cool winter period.

13. Olive (Olea europaea)

The Olive tree, with its gnarled trunk and evergreen leaves, is a symbol of peace and vitality. It is a sun-loving, drought-tolerant species, making it suitable for outdoor cultivation in warmer climates.

14. Trident Maple (Acer buergerianum)

The Trident Maple is a favorite among bonsai enthusiasts for its stunning autumn colors and unique root structures. It requires outdoor cultivation with a period of winter dormancy.

15. Willow (Salix)

Willows are often styled in the weeping form, with long, slender branches that hang down towards the ground. They prefer a lot of water and sunlight and are suitable for outdoor cultivation.

16. Hawthorn (Crataegus)

Hawthorn is known for its lovely spring blossoms and autumn fruits. It's a hardy species that can withstand a variety of conditions, making it a good choice for outdoor bonsai.

17.Hornbeam (Carpinus)

Hornbeams are favored for their beautiful leaf textures and autumn colors. Both European and Korean varieties are popular in bonsai. They require outdoor conditions and a cool winter period.

18.Zelkova (Zelkova serrata)

Often mistaken for Elms due to their similar leaf shape, Zelkovas are known for their gorgeous autumn foliage. They make excellent outdoor bonsai and prefer a winter dormancy period.

19.Yew (Taxus)

Yews are versatile evergreen trees with dark green needles. They can be designed into a variety of styles and are often used for deadwood bonsai techniques. They require outdoor cultivation.

20.Cedar (Cedrus)

Cedars are evergreen conifers with beautiful wood and distinctive needle clusters. They prefer outdoor conditions and can be styled in many ways, including formal upright and group plantings.

Remember that each tree species has specific care needs, and understanding these is crucial to its health and growth. Your local climate and environment will also play a significant role in determining which species will thrive. As you gain experience, you may want to try working with different species to challenge your skills and enrich your bonsai practice.

Glossary of Bonsai Terms

Bonsai cultivation comes with its own set of terms and jargon. Understanding these terms can enhance your comprehension and practice of this ancient art form. Here are some commonly used bonsai terms:

- **Apex:** The highest point or topmost part of a bonsai tree.

- **Bonsai:** A Japanese art form of growing and styling miniature trees in containers, literally meaning "planted in a container".

- **Bud:** A compact growth on a plant that develops into a leaf, branch, or flower.

- **Cascade Style (Kengai):** A bonsai style where the tree's branches and trunk fall beneath the base of the pot, mimicking a tree growing on a steep cliff.

- **Conifer:** A type of tree that produces cones and typically has needle-like or scale-like leaves. Many conifers are evergreen.

- **Deciduous:** Trees or shrubs that lose their leaves annually.

- **Evergreen:** Trees or shrubs that retain their leaves throughout the year.

- **Formal Upright Style (Chokkan):** A style of bonsai where the tree grows straight up with a single trunk.

- **Grafting:** A horticultural technique whereby tissues from one plant are inserted into those of another so that the two sets of vascular tissues may join together.

- **Group Planting (Ikadabuki):** A style of bonsai where multiple trees are planted together in a single pot to mimic a forest or cluster of trees.

- **Internode:** The part of a plant stem between two of the nodes (where leaves are attached).

- **Jin:** A technique in bonsai aesthetics that involves creating the appearance of a dead or broken branch.

- **Literati Style (Bunjin):** A bonsai style that represents a tree's struggle to reach light while contending with harsh weather conditions, resulting in a twisted and contorted form.

- **Nebari:** The surface roots of a bonsai tree.

- **Node:** The part of a plant stem from which one or more leaves emerge, often forming a slight swelling or knob.

- **Pruning:** The process of trimming a tree or shrub to remove unwanted parts, control growth, or shape the plant.

- **Root Pruning:** The act of trimming the roots of a plant to encourage more compact root growth.

- **Shari:** A bonsai technique that involves stripping away the bark from a section of the tree's trunk to mimic natural wear and aging.

- **Yamadori:** The practice of collecting tree specimens from the wild to be cultivated as bonsai.

- **Wiring:** A common bonsai technique involving wrapping wire around the branches of a tree to manipulate its shape and direction of growth.

Bonsai cultivation is as much about the journey as it is about the end result. Understanding these terms can provide a deeper insight into the art of bonsai and enhance your enjoyment of this peaceful and rewarding hobby.

Printed in Great Britain
by Amazon